Religions of the World

Judaism

Sue Penney

Heinemann
LIBRARY

H www.heinemann.co.uk/library
Visit our website to find out more information about Heinemann Library books.

To order:
☎ Phone 44 (0) 1865 888066
▤ Send a fax to 44 (0) 1865 314091
▢ Visit the Heinemann Bookshop at www.heinemann.co.uk/library to browse our catalogue and order online.

First published in Great Britain by Heinemann Library, Halley Court, Jordan Hill, Oxford
OX2 8EJ, a division of Reed Educational and Professional Publishing Ltd. Heinemann is a registered trademark of Reed
Educational & Professional Publishing Limited.

OXFORD MELBOURNE AUCKLAND JOHANNESBURG BLANTYRE
GABORONE IBADAN PORTSMOUTH NH (USA) CHICAGO

Designed by Ken Vail Graphic Design
Originated by Universal
Printed by Wing King Tong in Hong Kong.

ISBN 0 431 14954 2 (hardback)   ISBN 0 431 14961 5 (paperback)
06 05 04 03   07 06 05 04 03
10 9 8 7 6 5 4 3 2   10 9 8 7 6 5 4 3 2 1

British Library Cataloguing in Publication Data

Penney, Sue
Judaism. – (Religions of the world)
1. Judaism – Juvenile literature
1. Title
296

Acknowledgements
The Publishers would like to thank the following for permission to reproduce photographs:
AKG/Erich Lessing p. 9; Ancient Art and Architecture p. 24; Andes Press Agency/Carlos Reyes-Manzo p. 26a; Carlos
Reyes-Manzo, Andes Press Agency pp. 39, 42; Circa Photo Library pp. 16, 28, /Barrie Searle pp. 7, 12, 22, 37, /John Smith
p. 15, /Zbigniew Kosc p. 41; Collections/ Mike Kipling p. 10; Impact Photos /Robin Laurance p. 23, /Rachel Morton p 13,
/Steward Weir p. 20; John T. Hopf p.25; Juliette Soester pp. 5, 18, 30, 34, 36; Peter Osborne, p. 29; Photoedit pp. 19, 35,
43; The Stock Market pp.17, 21; Topham Picturepoint p. 11; Zev Radovan pp 4, 6, 14, 26b, 27, 31, 32.

Cover photograph reproduced with permission of Sonia Halliday/Barry Searle.

Our thanks to Philip Emmett for his comments in the preparation of this book.

Every effort has been made to contact copyright holders of any material reproduced in this book. Any omissions will be
rectified in subsequent printings if notice is given to the Publisher.

Any words appearing in the text in bold, **like this**, are explained in the Glossary.

Contents

Dates: in this book, dates are followed by the letters BCE (Before Common Era) or CE (Common Era). This is instead of using BC (Before Christ) and AD (*Anno Domini*, meaning In the year of our Lord), which is a Christian system. The date numbers are the same in both systems.

Introducing Judaism

Judaism is one of the oldest religions of the world. The people who follow it are called Jews.

What do Jews believe?

Jews believe that there is one God. They believe that God

A Jewish family in Jerusalem, Israel.

is a **spirit**. Jews do not believe that God is male or female, but they usually refer to God as 'he'. Jews believe that God made everything, and cares about what he made. He is so holy that Jews never use his name. They often use the word **Adonai** instead. This means 'Lord'.

The Covenant

Jews believe that they have a special relationship with God. They believe that they are God's Chosen People. This is because of a special agreement which Jews believe they have with God. This is called the Covenant. Jews believe this means that they have a duty to obey the rules which God has given them. These are written down in the part of the Jewish holy books which is called the **Torah**. God's side of the Covenant is that God will take care of the Jews.

The Jewish family

Today, Jews live all over the world. However, the fact that they are Jews is very important to them. They think of themselves as like one big family. Just like a family, they do not always agree with each other about everything, but their relationship is very important. Most Jews today feel that they share something important with other Jews, even if they live in countries where everyday life is quite different.

A group of young Jews outside a synagogue in London.

Facts about Judaism

- *Judaism began about 4000 years ago.*
- *Jews worship one God. They often call God Adonai.*
- *The Jewish place of worship is called a **synagogue**. Jews often call it shul.*
- *The most important Jewish holy books are called the Torah, (Books of Teaching). When they are used in the synagogue, they are written on a **scroll**. This is like a book with one long page, which is wound around rollers at both ends.*
- *There are two **symbols** for Judaism. One is a star with six points. This is called the Star of David or the Shield of David. The other is a candlestick with seven branches. It is called a **menorah**.*
- *There are about 13 million Jews in the world today.*

Abraham and Moses

Jews believe that in the early days of Judaism two men, Abraham and Moses, were very important leaders. Their stories are found in the **Torah**, part of the Jewish holy books.

Abraham

You can find the places mentioned in this book on the map on page 44.

Abraham lived in a beautiful city called Ur, in the country that today we call Iraq. The people there worshipped gods of the sun and the moon. Abraham felt this was wrong. He believed there was another God who was more important. Abraham felt that this God was telling him to leave Ur. So, with his wife and his family, Abraham set out on a journey. He believed that God was leading him. Jews believe that God led Abraham to the country that we call Israel. There God promised that he would care for Abraham's children, and their children, for ever.

This picture shows the sort of country that Jews believe both Abraham and Moses travelled through. It still looks the same today.

Moses

Hundreds of years after the time of Abraham, the Jews were living in Egypt. They became slaves who were very badly treated by the Egyptian ruler, called the **Pharaoh**. Moses believed that God wanted him to rescue the Jews.

*The first words of the Ten Commandments, written in **Hebrew**, the language of the Jews.*

Moses went to see the Pharaoh. He warned that disasters would happen in Egypt if the Jews were not allowed to return to their own country, which they called Canaan. The Pharaoh refused to let them go, because he did not want to lose the slaves who were working for him.

Jews believe that ten disasters happened, just as Moses had said they would. At last the Pharaoh agreed that the Jews could go. Moses led them out of Egypt. He was their leader for 40 years as they travelled back to Canaan, which today is called Israel. During this time, the Torah says, God gave Moses a set of rules that the Jews should obey. They are called the Ten **Commandments**.

The Ten Commandments

1. *You must not have any gods but me.*
2. *Do not make any **idols** to worship.*
3. *Do not use God's name carelessly.*
4. *Keep the **Sabbath** special.*
5. *Respect your father and mother.*
6. *Do not kill.*
7. *Do not take part in **adultery**.*
8. *Do not steal.*
9. *Do not tell lies about people.*
10. *Do not be jealous of what other people have.*

The early days of Judaism

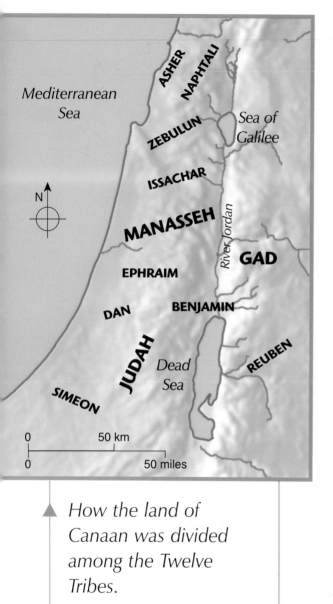

How the land of Canaan was divided among the Twelve Tribes.

Jews believe that Judaism began when God led Abraham to Canaan, which is the country now called Israel. When Abraham's grandson was alive, the **Torah** says, there was a famine. This meant that there was no food in Canaan. The Jews moved to Egypt, where there was food. They lived there for hundreds of years. Then a new **Pharaoh** (ruler) came to power. He was worried about so many Jews living in his country, and so he made them work as slaves. After many years, Moses rescued the Jews, and led them back to Canaan.

Other people were living in Canaan, and the Jews had to fight to take control. Then the land was divided up among groups of Jews, called the Twelve **Tribes**. Each tribe had a different name. Their leaders were called Judges. The tribes were not very united. After many years they agreed to have a king, who would rule them all. The first king was called Saul.

Kings

The Jews were ruled by kings for many years. The second king was called David. The Torah tells the story of how when he was a boy, David killed a giant called Goliath. When he became king David ruled wisely. Canaan became rich and successful. Many Jews look back to this time as the best time in their history.

When David died, his son Solomon became king. A magnificent **Temple** was built where God could be worshipped. When King Solomon died Canaan divided. The northern part became the kingdom of Israel. The southern part became the kingdom of Judah. After about 200 years, an army from the country of Assyria took over the kingdom of Israel. Many people were taken to live in Assyria, and Israel was destroyed.

About 100 years later, another great country, Babylon, invaded the kingdom of Judah. Again, people were taken away and Judah was almost destroyed.

In 538 BCE Cyrus the Great of Persia conquered Babylon. He allowed all the people who had been made to live in Babylon to return to their home country if they wished. Some Jews chose to return to Judah, but most chose to stay in Babylon.

This is what the entrance to Babylon would have looked like when the Jews were taken there from Judah.

The Diaspora

The Diaspora is the name for Jews living in other countries. Many times in Jewish history, people have been made to move, or have chosen to go and live in another country rather than be ruled by enemies.

Persecution

In 1190 CE, 150 Jews died in this castle in York.

Persecution means being punished for what you believe. Jews have been persecuted many times in their history. For hundreds of years from the late sixth century CE, Jews were not even allowed to live in some countries. In other places, they were made to live in particular areas, where they could be locked in behind gates at night.

The Holocaust

The worst persecution of Jews happened in the 1930s and 1940s when **Nazis** were in power in Germany. Jews had to wear a yellow star on their clothes so they could be recognized in the street. New laws said that Jews could not own cars. Jews could not ride on buses or trains. Jewish children could not go to school. Jews could not be outside after 9 o'clock at night. The list went on and on. Their lives became much harder.

Then the Nazis decided to get rid of Jews completely. Jews were taken away to special prisons, called concentration camps. Many were killed immediately. Others were starved and beaten before they were killed. They were not given enough clothes to wear and their hair was shaved off. By 1945, more than six million Jews had been killed. One and a half million of them were children. This was one in every three Jews in the world. The name given to these events is the **Holocaust**.

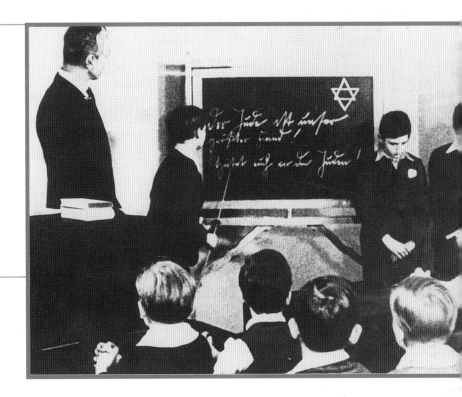

After World War II

After World War II, a new country, called Israel, was given to Jews. Jews had not had a country of their own for many hundreds of years. However, Arab people who were already living in the land of the Jews did not want Jews to live there. Because of this, Israel had wars with many countries around it during the twentieth century. There were major wars in 1956, 1967 and 1973. Recently, some peace agreements have been signed, but it is difficult to get everyone to agree when people feel so strongly.

Anne Frank
Anne Frank's family were Jews. During World War II they went into hiding. For over two years, they lived in secret rooms. Anne kept a diary about their life. Then someone told the Nazis where they were hiding. The family were taken to prison camps. Anne, her sister and her mother all died. After the war, Anne's father published her diary.

Different groups in Judaism

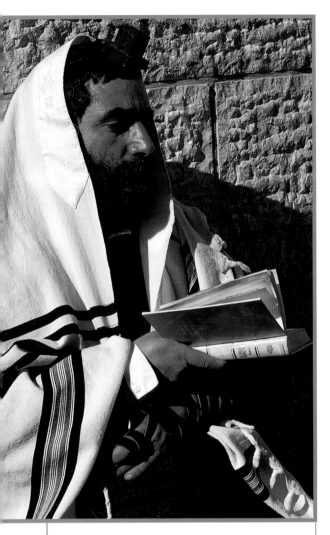

An Orthodox Jew wearing special clothes for worship.

Every religion is made up of different people. They all have their own opinions. They all share the most important beliefs, but something that matters very much to one member of the religion may not matter so much to another. This is the reason why different groups live in different ways, even when they all follow the same religion. Followers of Judaism all believe the basic teachings, but different groups of Jews do not agree about other parts of the religion.

Jews today may belong to one of many groups. The two main groups of Jews today are **Orthodox** Jews and **Progressive** Jews.

Orthodox Jews

More Jews today belong to the Orthodox group than to any other group. In the UK, about three Jews in every four are Orthodox.

Orthodox Jews believe that the **Torah** (the first part of the Jewish holy books) is the word of God. They believe that it tells people what God wants and how God wants them to live. Orthodox Jews believe that the Torah should never be changed, so that Jews can know what God wants whenever and wherever they live.

Progressive Jews

There are several groups of Progressive Jews. Most of these groups have begun in the last 200 years. They all believe that Judaism can be changed to fit different circumstances.

Progressive Jews do not keep the rules of the Torah as strictly as Orthodox Jews. They believe that if a rule does not seem to have a point any more, it can be changed or forgotten. When changes are made they often make life easier for Progressive Jews who live among people who are not Jews.

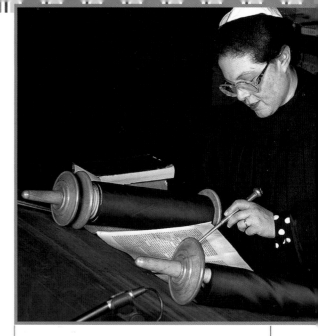

▲ Progressive Jews allow women to become **rabbis**. This is Rabbi Tabbick, who works in London.

ORTHODOX JEWS	PROGRESSIVE JEWS
In the synagogue	
• *Men wear special clothes for worship*	• *Men do not wear special clothes*
• *Women sit away from men*	• *Men and women sit together*
• *Men always lead the worship*	• *Men and women can take equal part*
• *Worship is always in the* **Hebrew** *language*	• *Worship is usually in everyday language*
At home	
• **Sabbath** *is a day of total rest*	• *No paid work done on Sabbath*
• **Kosher** *food rules kept strictly*	• *Kosher food rules not kept strictly*
• *Someone is counted as Jewish only if his or her mother was a Jew*	• *Someone is Jewish if either parent was a Jew, or if he or she was brought up as a Jew*

Jewish holy books

Jewish holy books are divided into three parts. The first is the Books of Teaching, called the **Torah**. The second is the Books of the **Prophets**. The third is the Books of Writings.

The Torah

The Torah is the most important part of the Jewish holy books. Torah means the Books of Teaching. They contain the rules which teach Jews how they should live. There are 613 rules, about all parts of life. Some Jews keep the rules more carefully than others. Many Jews try to keep them all, because they believe the rules show how God wants them to live. In other parts of the Torah, there are stories about how the world was made, and about the very first Jews. For reading in the **synagogue**, the books of the Torah are written on **scrolls**.

The Books of the Prophets

A prophet is someone who tells people what God wants. Jews believe that the prophets were men and women who were given special powers by God so they could tell people how God wanted them to live. Jews believe that what the prophets said is still important for Jews today.

An open scroll, showing the rollers at each end.

The Books of Writings

The Books of Writings contain stories from Jewish history. The book used most often in worship is the Book of **Psalms**. A psalm is a sort of poem, and can be used like a song. Many of the psalms are supposed to have been written by King David. Parts of the Books of Writings are read at particular festivals. For example, the Book of Esther is always read at Purim.

Reading the Torah in the synagogue. The silver pointer is called a yad.

Scrolls

*A scroll is like a book with one long page. It is made of **parchment**. A complete scroll is about 60 metres long when it is unwound. Every scroll is written by hand. The **scribes** who write them are specially trained. They use a special ink and pen. Scrolls are treated with great care. They are never touched by anyone's hands. When they are being read in the synagogue, a pointer called a yad is used to help the person who is reading to follow the words on the scroll.*

What the holy books say

The holy books tell the story of thousands of years of Jewish history, and the Jews' relationship with God. They also tell what the Jews learned about God.

The Shema

The **Shema** is the most important Jewish prayer. It is found in the fifth book of the **Torah**, which is called the Book of Deuteronomy. It reminds Jews how important it is to love God. These words are from the Shema:

Hear, Israel, the Lord is our God. The Lord is one. Now you must love the Lord your God with all your heart and with all your soul and with all your strength. And these words which I am commanding you today shall be upon your heart. … And you must bind them as a sign upon your arm and they shall be a token between your eyes. And you must write them on the doorposts of your house and on your gates.
(Deuteronomy 6: 4–9)

Many Jews follow these rules by wearing special leather boxes on their arm and forehead when they are dressed for worship. They also have a special **scroll**, called a **mezuzah**, on their doors. They touch this as they go in and out, to remind them of what God taught.

This is a **scribe** writing the Shema on a mezuzah scroll.

The prophets

Other important books for Jews are the Books of the **Prophets**. Jews believe that prophets gave the Jews important messages from God. For example, two prophets called Micah and Hosea told the people how they should live:

This is what the Lord asks of you: to do justice and love mercy and walk humbly with your God. (Micah 6: 8)
(The Lord says) I desire goodness and not sacrifices, and the knowledge of God rather than burnt offerings. (Hosea 6: 6)

Another prophet, Isaiah, looked forward to a time when people would live as God wanted:

They shall beat their swords into ploughshares and their spears into pruning hooks. Nation shall not lift up sword against nation, nor shall they practise for war any more. (Isaiah 2: 4)

These words from the Book of Isaiah are still very important, even for people who are not Jews. They are carved on the main building of the United Nations. The United Nations is an international organization which helps different countries to work together in peace.

The main building of the United Nations in New York, USA.

Worship at home

Mezuzah

Jews believe that every part of their life is part of their worship. One way that they remind themselves of this is by touching a **mezuzah** as they go in or out of a room. A mezuzah is a tiny **scroll** which has the first two paragraphs of a Jewish prayer, the **Shema**, written on it. It fits inside a special case, which is fixed to the right-hand side of a doorpost. Touching the mezuzah on their way in and out of a room reminds Jews that God is always there.

This mezuzah is by the front door of a Jewish home.

Sabbath

The Jewish **Sabbath** lasts from sunset on a Friday until sunset on a Saturday. (All Jewish days are counted from sunset to sunset.) It is a special day of rest and worship for Jews. It begins when the wife or mother in the family lights two candles and says a prayer which welcomes the Sabbath. After a service at the **synagogue**, Jewish families meet for the Sabbath eve meal. This always includes special bread called **challah bread**. It is a relaxed and happy meal when the family can be together.

Lighting the candles means that the Sabbath has begun.

On the Sabbath itself, **Orthodox** Jews do not work. This does not just mean not going to work. It also includes other types of work, such as cooking (food is prepared the day before), driving, shopping and so on. This means that the Sabbath is a day when Jews can relax at home or with friends without feeling that they have to rush around and get on with life.

The Sabbath ends with a special ceremony called the **havdalah**, when Jews light a plaited candle and everyone smells a box of spices. They hope that the peace of the Sabbath will spread through the coming week just like the smell of the spices spreads through the house. After they have said a prayer, the candle is put out by dipping it in a cup of wine. The sabbath is over when three stars can be seen in the sky.

Why Jews celebrate the Sabbath

*The **Torah** says that God created the world in six days and rested on the seventh day. Because of this, Jews have always kept the Sabbath – the seventh day – as a day of rest. They believe that the Sabbath is very important. They see it as a special gift from God. They sometimes call it Queen Sabbath.*

Worship in the synagogue

When Jews worship God, they pray and they ask God for help in their lives. They thank God for the things he has done for them. Jews believe that they can worship God anywhere, but the **synagogue** is a special place where they can meet and worship together. Jews do not often use the word synagogue. Sometimes they call it shul (it rhymes with rule).

Synagogue service

A service is a special meeting for worship. A synagogue service includes readings from the Jewish holy books, prayers and singing of **psalms**, which are like poems. On the **Sabbath**, music is not played with the singing, because Jews believe this is a form of work. On other days, music may be played. During the service there is usually a talk, so people can learn more about Judaism. At some services, there are readings from the **Torah**.

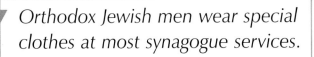
▼ *Orthodox Jewish men wear special clothes at most synagogue services.*

Special clothes

Men usually wear a special cap called a **kippah** in the synagogue. Jews believe that this shows respect for God. Some Jewish men wear a kippah all the time. At morning services, men wear a **tallit**, too. This is a prayer robe, rather like a scarf. It is usually made of silk or wool, and has fringes at each end. A tallit is about 2 metres long and 1.5 metres wide.

This rabbi is inspecting the tiny scroll from the inside of a tefillah to make sure it is not damaged in any way.

For some services in an **Orthodox** synagogue, men may wear two small black leather boxes which have long straps. They are called **tefillin** (where there is only one it is called a **tefillah**). They wear them because they believe that God told them to do so in the **Shema**, the special Jewish prayer. One tefillah is worn in the middle of the forehead, reminding them to love God with all their mind. The other tefillah is fastened to their arm, facing their heart, reminding them to love God with all their heart. The boxes contain tiny **scrolls** with short pieces of writing from the Torah.

Rabbis

*A **rabbi** is a teacher and leader for Jews. Rabbis are very respected by other Jews because they have studied the Torah and other Jewish holy books, and they know a great deal about Judaism. Many rabbis lead classes to teach Jews about Judaism and the Torah. In the synagogue services, the rabbi often leads the prayers, and may also give a talk. A rabbi also conducts wedding and funeral services. In Orthodox synagogues, only men become rabbis. In **Progressive** synagogues, women may become rabbis, too.*

The synagogue

The **synagogue** is the place where Jews meet to worship God. Synagogues all over the world look very similar inside, although the outside may look different. Synagogues usually have a Star of David outside, and there is often **Hebrew** writing above the door.

The Holy Ark

At the front of the main room in the synagogue is a special cupboard. It is called the **Holy Ark**, and it contains the **scrolls** on which the **Torah** is written. The scrolls are taken out of the Holy Ark to be read during worship. They are carried carefully from the Holy Ark to the reading desk.

When they are put away in the Holy Ark, the scrolls are wrapped in beautiful covers. The cover is called a **mantle**. Mantles are often made of silk or velvet. In some Jewish groups mantles may be made of wood or metal. They are always beautifully decorated. The scrolls are also decorated with a crown and bells which are at the end of the wooden rollers. These help to remind Jews that the scrolls are very important. Next to the Holy Ark there is often a seat for the **rabbi** who leads the synagogue services.

These scrolls in their mantles are being kept inside the Holy Ark until they are needed in a service.

The ner tamid

In front of the Holy Ark is a special lamp, called the **ner tamid**. The flame is kept burning all the time. The ner tamid reminds Jews that God is always with them. It is also a reminder of the lamp in the **Temple** which was never allowed to go out.

The bimah

The **bimah** is a raised part of the floor in front of the Holy Ark or in the middle of the synagogue. It has a reading desk where the Torah is placed when it is going to be read. The person who is leading the service may stand on the bimah. Sometimes they stand at the front of the synagogue, instead.

The women's section

In **Orthodox** synagogues, men and women do not sit together. Women have a separate section of their own, where they sit with young children. This may be at one end of the synagogue, or upstairs. In **Progressive** synagogues, everyone sits together.

▼ *Orthodox Jewish teenagers meeting at a summer camp in the USA.*

Learning about Judaism

*Jews believe that learning about Judaism is important. There is usually at least one room in the synagogue where classes can be held. People learn about the Torah and other holy books. Children learn the **Hebrew** language. Young Jews from different areas or even different countries may meet at the synagogue or in other places.*

Places of worship

The Temple

In the early days of Judaism, the **Temple** in Jerusalem was the centre of the Jewish religion. For hundreds of years, Jews believed that it was the only place where they could worship God properly. The first Temple was built in the time of King Solomon, about 960 BCE. It took seven years to build, and was one of the most splendid buildings in the world.

You can find the places mentioned in this book on the map on page 44.

In the first century CE, the Jews' country was called Palestine. At that time, the Romans ruled much of the world, including Palestine. In 66 CE, the Jews in Palestine fought against the Roman rulers. The Romans won the battle. Because the Temple was so important to the Jews, the Romans wanted to destroy it. In 70 CE, they burnt it to the ground. Only one wall was left standing. All the Temple treasures which were made of gold and silver were taken to Rome. Every year, Jews remember the day on which the Temple was destroyed. It is one of the saddest days of the year for Jews. The one wall which was left is still standing today. It is called the Western Wall, and many Jews go there to pray.

This picture was carved in Rome just after the Jewish Temple in Jerusalem had been destroyed. It shows soldiers carrying the Temple treasures back to Rome.

The Touro synagogue

The Touro **synagogue** is famous because it is the oldest synagogue in the USA. It was built in 1759 and is beautifully decorated. The women's section is upstairs and is supported by twelve columns. Each column is made of a single tree trunk. The twelve columns are to remind Jews of the Twelve **Tribes** of Israel.

Prayer on entering the synagogue

When they enter a synagogue, Jews say a special prayer. It includes the words:

Due to your great kindness I will come into your house… Lord, I love the dwelling of your house, and the place where your glory rests.

The Jews who built the Touro synagogue had travelled to the USA because they were being **persecuted** where they lived in Europe. They must have still been afraid that they were going to be attacked, because underneath the **bimah** in the synagogue there is a trapdoor. This would have allowed them to escape if enemies came to the synagogue. Today the synagogue is still used as a place of worship. It is also a place which thousands of people come to visit and admire.

Inside the Touro synagogue. Notice the bimah in the middle, and the women's gallery upstairs.

Pilgrimage

A **pilgrimage** is a journey which someone makes because of their religion. A pilgrim may go to the place where the religion began, or to somewhere else that is important.

You can find the places mentioned in this book on the map on page 44.

The Western Wall

The Western Wall is the most important place of pilgrimage for Jews. It is in Jerusalem, and it is all that remains of the old Jewish **Temple**. Jews today go to the Western Wall to pray. As well as saying their prayers, they often put small pieces of paper with prayers written on them into the spaces between the stones. A service is held every day at the Western Wall, where Jews can pray together. The rest of the area which was covered by the Temple is now the place where the **Muslim** Mosque of the Dome of the Rock stands.

The Western Wall is all that stands of the Jewish Temple which was destroyed by the Romans in 70 CE. Pilgrims today place prayers written on small pieces of paper between the stones. You can see this in the top photo.

Yad Vashem

Yad Vashem is another important place for Jewish pilgrims. It is also in Jerusalem, in a place called the Mount of Remembrance. Yad Vashem was set up in 1953 to remember the six million Jews who were killed in the **Holocaust** during World War II.

Yad Vashem has pictures and displays showing some of the dreadful things which happened to Jews in the German prisons known as concentration camps. Another part of Yad Vashem is a special place where people can spend time thinking about those who died. Most Jews who are alive today know that members of their family were killed during World War II. In another part, specially planted trees and names on a wall remember people who put their lives in danger helping Jews to escape from the Germans. More than 16,000 people are remembered there.

Remembering those who died

In Israel, 27th Nisan (the seventh month of the Jewish year) is a day to remember Jews who died in the Holocaust. This makes it a special day for people to visit Yad Vashem.

This sculpture is part of Yad Vashem. It helps people to remember the Jews who died in the Holocaust.

Celebrating Rosh Hashanah and Yom Kippur

Rosh Hashanah

Rosh Hashanah is the Jewish New Year. On the evening before Rosh Hashanah, Jews eat a special meal. It includes pieces of apple dipped in honey. This is a way of saying that they hope the year that is beginning will be sweet and happy. On Rosh Hashanah, there is a special service in the **synagogue**. The **shofar** is blown 100 times. A shofar is a musical instrument made from a ram's horn. It plays two notes and sounds a bit like a trumpet. It reminds Jews that God is very important.

In some places, Jewish families go for a walk after lunch on Rosh Hashanah. They walk to a river or other running water. They empty crumbs from their pockets, and throw them into the water. The crumbs are carried away by the water. This is a **symbol** to show that Jews hope their sins will be forgiven.

▲ *The shofar is made from a ram's horn.*

The Days of Returning

Rosh Hashanah is the first of ten special days for Jews. They are called the Days of Returning. During this time, Jews think about everything they have done wrong in the past year. They try to make up any quarrels and make sure their life is all in order. Then they are ready to 'return' to God at Yom Kippur. This means that they feel close to God again.

At Yom Kippur everyone wears white. Men wear a white robe like this one over their clothes.

Yom Kippur

The tenth Day of Returning is called Yom Kippur. This is a special day when Jews ask God to forgive them for everything they have done wrong. They spend a lot of the day in the synagogue, and they **fast** for 25 hours. They believe that this shows how sorry they are for the things they have done wrong. Jews believe that God will forgive them if they are really sorry, so at Yom Kippur they also remember how much God loves them.

At the end of the service, the shofar is blown again. This is to remind people of all the good things they have promised they will do in the year ahead.

The Jewish calendar

*Jews believe that the **Torah** tells them when God made the world. The Jewish calendar counts years from that time. This is 3761 years ahead of the Western calendar. The Western calendar counts years from the birth of Jesus Christ. The Jewish year begins in September or early October. For example, the Jewish year 5766 will begin in September 2005. Jewish months start at the new moon and last for 29 or 30 days. Every three years, there is an extra month so that the months always occur in the same season. Festivals are celebrated on the same date in the Jewish calendar every year.*

Celebrating Pesach (Passover)

The story of Pesach

Pesach is one of the most important Jewish festivals. At Pesach, Jews remember the story in the **Torah** of how Moses led the Jews to freedom after they had been slaves in Egypt. The story tells that ten disasters happened in Egypt before the Egyptian **Pharaoh** agreed to free the Jews. During the tenth disaster, the eldest son in every Egyptian family died. To protect themselves from this disaster the Jews put lamb's blood on their doorposts. This meant that that the Angel of Death would pass over their houses.

When bread is made, people use some sort of leaven, for example yeast or self-raising flour, to make the bread rise (grow). The Torah tells that when the Jews left Egypt, they went so quickly that they could not wait for their bread to rise. To remember this, at Pesach Jews always eat **unleavened** (flat) bread.

Before Pesach, the house is searched for leaven, sometimes using a candle and a feather. Even small crumbs are removed.

Celebrating Pesach

Pesach lasts for eight days. In that time, Jews have no contact with anything that contains leaven. The main part of the celebrations is the **Seder** – the Pesach meal. During the meal, the youngest person present at the Seder asks four questions. The oldest person present at the Seder answers them. The answers tell the story of the first Pesach.

The Seder includes both ordinary food and foods which have a special meaning. Special foods are put on the Seder plate. There is a lamb bone, a reminder of the lambs killed in Egypt; a hard-boiled egg, a symbol of new life; a green vegetable, a symbol of how God looked after the Jews; bitter herbs, a reminder of how unhappy they were in Egypt; and charoset (a sweet paste made of nuts and apples), a reminder of the sweetness of freedom.

There is also a plate of matzoh (flat crackers of unleavened bread), a bowl of salt water (a symbol of tears) and a glass of wine for each person. Wine is drunk four times during the meal, to remember that God promised four times to bring the Jews out of Egypt.

A song for Pesach

Jews often sing songs at Pesach. A popular one fits the tune of Green Grow The Rushes, Oh! *It begins,*

Who knows what one
   is, now our Seder's
   finishing?
I know what one is:
One is God for
   evermore on earth and
   up in heaven.

▲ *The Seder plate contains five special things to remind Jews of the story of the escape from Egypt.*

Celebrating Sukkot

A **sukkah** is a sort of hut. (**Sukkot** is the word for more than one sukkah.) Jews build sukkot to remember how Jews lived thousands of years ago. After they escaped from Egypt, Jews lived in the desert for many years. Some probably had tents, but many of the people had to build themselves somewhere to live. They built sukkot.

The lulav

At **synagogue** services during the week of Sukkot, Jewish men hold a **lulav**. This is made of branches from three types of tree – palm, willow and myrtle. The lulav is held in the left hand. In their right hand, the men hold a citron. A citron is a fruit rather like a lemon.

▼ *Some sukkot are big enough for everyone who goes to the synagogue.*

How to build a sukkah

A sukkah is usually made of wood. The most important part is the roof. It is covered in leaves or branches, but it must be left open enough to be able to see the sky. The roof is often decorated with fruit. It may have electric lights, too.

During the services, men walk around the **bimah** carrying the citron and waving the lulav. The lulav and the citron are **symbols** – something that has a deeper meaning. The palm is a symbol of the spine. The willow is a symbol of the lips. The myrtle is a symbol of the eyes. The citron is a symbol of the heart. Together, they remind Jews that they must worship God with all their body. The lulav are also waved in every direction – up, down, forward, back and left and right. This is a symbol that God rules all the universe.

Simchat Torah

Simchat Torah is the day after the end of Sukkot. It is a day when Jews celebrate the **Torah**. Every week throughout the year, part of the Torah is read in the synagogue. Simchat Torah is the day when the very last part of the Torah is read, and the readings start from the beginning again. All the Torah **scrolls** are taken out of the **Holy Ark** and carried around the synagogue while the people sing and clap. It is a very happy day, and children are often given sweets and fruit as part of the celebrations.

At Simchat Torah everyone dances around the synagogue following the scrolls.

Celebrating Shavuot and Purim

Shavuot and Purim are both festivals which celebrate things that happened to the Jews many years ago. Shavuot is a more important festival than Purim.

Synagogues are decorated with fruit and flowers for the festival of Shavuot.

Shavuot

The festival of Shavuot celebrates the time when Jews believe God gave the Ten **Commandments** to Moses on a mountain called Mount Sinai. Before the festival, the **synagogue** is decorated with fruit and flowers. The **Torah** says that after God had spoken with Moses, flowers opened all over the mountain. At the synagogue service, the readings from the Torah tell the story of what happened. After the service, Jews celebrate with a meal at home. A special part of the meal is two loaves of bread which have the pattern of a ladder baked into them. This is to remind people that Moses had to climb the mountain to talk to God.

Purim

The story remembered at the festival of Purim happened hundreds of years ago in a country called Persia (now called Iran). A man called Haman helped the Persian king to rule Persia. Haman felt he was very important. He decided that everybody had to bow when he passed by.

Jews who were living in Persia at the time refused to do this, because to Jews bowing means worship, and they only worship God. Haman was very angry and made up an excuse to ask the king to order that all Jews in the country should be killed. The king agreed.

The king's wife, Queen Esther, heard about this. The king did not know it, but she was Jewish. Esther told the king the real reason why Haman wanted to kill the Jews. The king was very angry. He ordered that Haman should be killed instead. All the Jews were saved.

Celebrating Purim

At synagogue services, the story of Haman and Queen Esther is read out. Every time children hear Haman's name, they make as much noise as they can. They shout, whistle, stamp their feet and use special rattles called greggors. The idea is to make so much noise that no one can hear the name of the bad man Haman.

Celebrating Hanukkah

The story of Hanukkah

Almost 2000 years ago, the Jews' country, called Judah, had been taken over. The new king, Antiochus, was wicked and cruel. He would not allow Jews to worship God. He said they had to worship him instead!

A group of Jews fought against the king, led by a man called Judah the Maccabee. Judah's tiny army managed to beat the king's soldiers in battle. The Jews then had control of the city of Jerusalem. This was very important, because it was where the **Temple** was. The Temple was the most important place of worship for Jews. King Antiochus had spoiled the Temple. Judah wanted to make it fit for worship again.

The Temple was repaired and carefully cleaned. When it was ready, Judah went to light the **menorah**. This was the Temple lamp which was supposed to burn all the time. The king had let it go out. When Judah lit it again, it had only enough oil for one night. The oil was special, and it would take eight days to get some more. But the lamp stayed alight all the time! Jews believe that God made it burn because he was so pleased to be worshipped in the Temple again.

Hanukkah is a festival where even the youngest Jews can join in.

These Jewish children are playing the dreidle game.

Celebrating Hanukkah

Jews use a special candlestick to celebrate Hanukkah. It holds eight candles and an extra one which is used to light all the others. On the first night of the festival, Jews light one candle, on the second night they light two, and so on. As they light the candles, they say special prayers.

By the end of the festival all nine candles burn brightly. This shows that the Jews are remembering the miracle of how the oil lasted. Hanukkah is not one of the most important festivals, but it is a very happy time. People go to parties and give each other presents. They eat special foods like doughnuts (fried in oil) and latkes, which are potato cakes fried in oil.

A game for Hanukkah

*At Hanukkah children often play a game using a dreidle, which is like a spinning top with flat sides. On each side of the dreidle, there is a letter from the **Hebrew** alphabet. They are the first letters of words which say 'A great miracle happened here'. (Outside Israel, the last word is 'there'.)*

Special occasions – Bar Mitzvah and Bat Mitzvah

Bar mitzvah

Bar Mitzvah means 'son of the **commandments**'. It is a special service for boys. The Bar Mitzvah service takes place on the **Sabbath** following a Jewish boy's thirteenth birthday. For the first time, the boy can take part in the **synagogue** service. He says the prayer before the **Torah** is read. **Orthodox** Jews say this prayer in the **Hebrew** language. Some boys read a part of, or even the whole of, the day's reading from the Torah, too. The boy must practise hard so that he can say the Hebrew words perfectly, especially in front of lots of people! Often, his friends and relatives come to the service, and there may be a special meal afterwards.

Once he has reached this age, a Jewish boy is expected to obey all the Jewish rules. He is counted as a man. In Orthodox synagogues, a boy is often given his own **tefillin** for the first time for this service, so he has to learn how to put them on and tie the straps correctly.

This boy is celebrating his Bar Mitzvah at the Western Wall in Jerusalem.

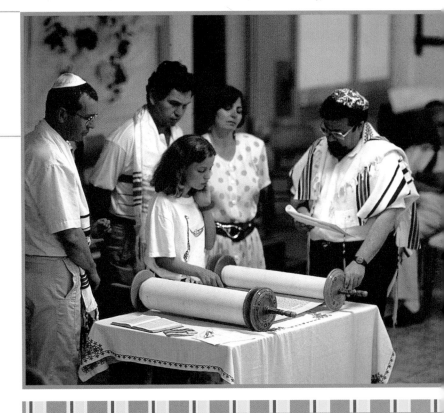

A Bat Mitzvah celebration in a Progressive synagogue.

Bat Mitzvah

Bat Mitzvah means 'daughter of the commandments'. Bat Mitzvah happens for a Jewish girl at the age of twelve. In **Progressive** synagogues, there is no difference between the services held for boys and girls. There is usually a party afterwards.

In Orthodox synagogues, a girl reaches Bat Mitzvah automatically. Not all Orthodox synagogues have special services for girls. If there is one, it is held on a Sunday rather than on the Sabbath. Girls do not read from the Torah in an Orthodox synagogue.

Bat Chayil

Bat Chayil means 'daughter of excellence'. It is another ceremony which many synagogues hold for girls. To prepare for Bat Chayil, the girl must learn more about Judaism. Many girls show what they have learned by doing a project. This often includes making something, as well as writing about what she has learned. During the ceremony, the girl reads some words in the Hebrew language. She is then welcomed by the people who meet at the synagogue for worship.

Special occasions – marriage and death

Marriage

Jews are expected to get married, and many Jews believe it is important to marry someone who is Jewish. They believe it is easier to share a life happily with someone who has been brought up to follow the same religion. Jewish weddings usually take place in a **synagogue**. In Israel, they are often held outdoors. The couple getting married are called the bride and the bridegroom. They stand under a covering called a **huppah**. The huppah may be decorated with flowers. It is a **symbol** of the home they will share.

▲ *An outdoor Jewish wedding in Israel.*

The **rabbi** leading the service says prayers over a glass of wine, then gives it to the bride and bridegroom to drink. Then the marriage promises are read out, in which the bridegroom agrees to look after his wife. The bridegroom gives the bride a ring, which she wears on the first finger of her right hand. There are more prayers, and at the end of the service, the bridegroom steps on a wine glass and breaks it. (It is carefully wrapped so it does not do any damage.) This is an old custom. It is a symbol that there may be bad things as well as good in their marriage. It is also a reminder that the Jewish **Temple** was destroyed all those years ago.

Divorce

Divorce is when a couple end their marriage. Jews allow divorce, but they make great efforts to avoid it. The only way a Jewish marriage can be ended is by a **get**. This is a special document written by a **scribe**. It gives details about the couple, and where and when they divorced.

Death

Jews believe that a funeral should be held as soon as possible after someone dies. It is usually held within 24 hours. Funeral services are very simple. Rich and poor are treated in exactly the same way. Bodies are buried and most Jews do not allow **cremation** because they think it destroys what God has made.

For a week after someone's funeral, their family do not leave the house except in an emergency. Friends come to visit them and say prayers. For one year after the death, **Orthodox** Jews do not listen to or play music (unless it is their job). Every year on the day the person died, close relatives burn a candle for a night and a day, and say special prayers.

After someone dies

A Jew's body must not be buried wearing make-up or fine clothes. The body is washed, and wrapped in a plain linen shroud. Then it is placed in a plain wooden coffin.

A place where Jews are buried on a hill opposite Jerusalem, Israel.

Ways to be a Jew

Jewish communities

Jews live all over the world. Many Jews choose to live in areas where there are other Jews. The rules about keeping the **Sabbath** mean that **Orthodox** Jews need to live where it is only a short walk to the **synagogue**. They need to attend Sabbath services, but they may not drive or have somebody else drive them there, because they believe this is a kind of work. Living in a community of Jews means that shops will be more likely to sell foods that Jews need to buy, for example, **kosher** foods. It also means that it is easy for them to spend time with other Jews – people who share their religion and ideas. Jews believe that this is especially important for young people, so they can grow up with others who share the same views.

Studying the holy books is an important part of life for Jews.

In the home

Jews believe that life as a family is very important. The customs they follow at home may have been handed down in the family for hundreds of years. Sometimes the Sabbath candlesticks or other things to do with the religion may have belonged to the family for years, too. Many Jews like the idea that they are continuing what Jews all over the world have done for thousands of years.

Being a Jew is much more than just going to a synagogue. It is a way of life. Jews believe that everything they do can be a way of serving God, if it is done properly.

▼ *Jews believe that preparing food properly is a way of serving God.*

Kosher foods

*Kosher means 'allowed' or 'suitable'. 'Keeping kosher' is important in many areas of Jewish life. Many Jews only eat kosher food. Some animals are not allowed as food, for example, pigs. Things that are not allowed are called **treifah**. To be kosher, an animal must be killed in a special way without suffering. Plants are kosher, but only if they are free from pests. Jews never eat meat and milk together. Jews believe that these are rules given by God. It is important to Jews that they follow these rules when preparing and eating the food which they believe God gave.*

Map

The globe on the right shows the location of the map below. The map shows some places that are important in the history of Judaism.

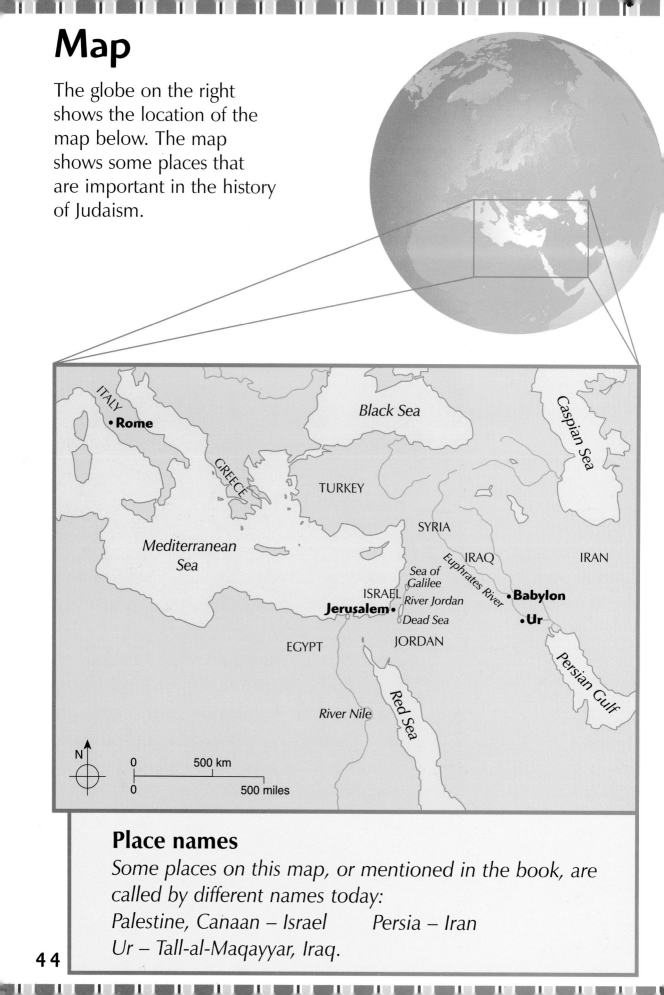

ITALY

• **Rome**

Black Sea

Caspian Sea

GREECE

TURKEY

Mediterranean Sea

SYRIA

IRAQ

IRAN

Euphrates River

Sea of Galilee

ISRAEL

River Jordan

• **Babylon**

Jerusalem •

Dead Sea

• **Ur**

EGYPT

JORDAN

Persian Gulf

River Nile

Red Sea

N

0

500 km

0

500 miles

Place names

Some places on this map, or mentioned in the book, are called by different names today:

Palestine, Canaan – Israel   Persia – Iran

Ur – Tall-al-Maqayyar, Iraq.

Timechart

Major events in World history

BCE	3000–1700	Indus valley civilization (Hinduism)
	c2685–1196	Egyptian civilization
	c2000	Abraham lived (Judaism)
	1800	Stonehenge completed
	c528	Siddhattha Buddha born (Buddhism)
	c450–146	Greek Empire
	200	Great Wall of China begun
	c300–300CE	Roman Empire
	c4	Jesus of Nazareth born (Christianity)
CE	570	Muhammad born (Islam)
	1066	Battle of Hastings and the Norman conquest of England
	1325–1521	Aztec Empire
	1400	Black Death kills one person in three in China, North Africa and Europe
	1469	Guru Nanak born (Sikhism)
	1564	William Shakespeare born
	1914–18	World War I
	1939–45	World War II
	1946	First computer invented
	1969	First moon landings
	2000	Millennium celebrations all over the world

Major events in Jewish history

BCE	c2000	Life of Abraham
	c1500	Life of Moses
	1500–1000	The time of the Judges
	1100	Saul becomes the Jews' first king
	922	Israel and Judah become separate kingdoms
	722	Army from Assyria conquers Israel
	586	Army from Babylon conquers Judah
	165	Judah the Maccabee rebels against Antiochus (Hanukkah)
	63	Romans conquer Palestine
CE	70	The Temple in Jerusalem is destroyed by the Romans
	1290	Jews are not allowed to live in England
	1818	First Progressive synagogue opened in Germany
	1880s	Persecution in Russia and Eastern countries leads to many Jews going to live in other countries
	1930s–40s	Persecution under Nazis in Germany and the Holocaust
	1948	The State of Israel is formed

Glossary

Adonai	'Lord' – Jewish name for God
adultery	sexual relations outside marriage
bimah	reading desk in a synagogue
challah bread	bread specially baked for the Sabbath
commandment	important rule
Covenant	special agreement between God and the Jews
cremation	burning a body after death
fast	go without food and drink for religious reasons
get	document which ends a Jewish marriage
havdalah	ceremony which ends the Sabbath
Hebrew	language of the Jews
Holy Ark	cupboard in the synagogue which contains the scrolls
Holocaust	name given to the killing of Jews during World War II
huppah	covering under which the bride and groom stand at a wedding
idol	statue or other false god
kippah	kind of cap worn by Jewish men
kosher	'allowed' – food which Jews are allowed to eat
lulav	collection of tree branches used at Sukkot
mantle	cover for a scroll
menorah	candlestick with seven branches
mezuzah	tiny scroll for placing on a doorpost
Muslim	follower of the religion of Islam
Nazi	rulers in Germany in the 1930s and 1940s
ner tamid	lamp in the synagogue which is never allowed to go out
Orthodox	group of Jews who follow traditional teachings
parchment	'paper' made of animal skin
persecution	being punished for what you believe
Pharaoh	king of Egypt

pilgrimage	journey which someone makes because of their religion
Progressive	groups of Jews who believe the traditional teachings of Judaism can be changed
prophet	man or woman who tells people what God wants
psalm	special poem used in worship
rabbi	Jewish teacher and leader
Sabbath	Jewish day of rest and worship
scribe	specially trained writer
scroll	rolled up 'book' on which the Torah is written
Seder	Passover meal
Shema	important Jewish prayer
shofar	instrument made from a ram's horn
spirit	being that does not have a body
sukkah	hut used during the festival of Sukkot
symbol	something which has a deep meaning
synagogue	Jewish place of worship
tallit	prayer robe worn by Jewish men
tefillin	leather boxes worn by Orthodox Jewish men (one is called a tefillah)
Temple	most important place of Jewish worship
Torah	Books of Teaching (first part of the Jewish holy books)
treifah	'not allowed' – food which Jews are not allowed to eat
Tribe	one of the twelve groups which the early Jews formed
unleavened	bread made without yeast or raising agent

Index